The Yolk of Getting Woke

Gabriel Lorenzo Mata

This book is for my son Jabril Luciano,
keep on shining my love.

Let the Children Dream

After a full day of learning

The brain must rest

The synapses are burning

The world is a treasure chest

Fully immersed so the wheels are turning

Until you hit the crest

A panoramic view of your earning

Then you use dreams as an express

Data to digest

To build knowledge and progress

Children's dreams become the world next

In our children's dreams we should invest

The Point of No Return

At certain tipping points the times must change,

like when the American founding minds waged war against a king.

It was time for society to rearrange no matter how strange.

The prospect of shedding monarchy into a people's democracy, let's see what it brings!

Culture always swings like wakes across lakes.

One day the people of Paris were so fed up they took to the streets,

to see if the neck of an aristocrat breaks.

They were starving so they stormed the Bastille and onward to Versailles.

The aristocrats kept eating their opulent cakes!

While the people had no bread and were willing to die,

for the idea that it was finally time.

Democracy had survived from ancient Greece and was about to go live!

Can you really stop an idea whose time has arrived?

Real Eyes

You read your Bible and your Koran

I hope you understand it was written by man

On this land

Wherever you stand

It is all up for interpretation

Opinions of mystics and politicians

Mystics read and write poetry like Rumi

Zealots interpret literally and war like Al-Baghdadi

The truth does not rest in the words, they are clues!

Behold a view like Lao Tzu's

Real Eyes it's inside of you!

Moksha, Nirvana, Godspeed, Christian, Muslim, Scientist, or Hindu

Atheist, Buddhist, Agnostic, Shaman, or Jew

The Great Spirit

Do you ever commune with the Great Spirit?

Nameless and yet you can hear it

The sound of DNA emitting photons

Your absolutes are nothing to rest on

All life is in motion

And you are part of the potion

Look outside and communicate with the trees and ants

DNA based life in a perfect dance

Essentially your DNA is made the same as all DNA based life

Like the shaman's food teaches you that nature is your wife

Fall into a trance and notice the molecular biology

And you might realize that all things emit a frequency

The ancients taught us the path to commune

Don't get caught up in what makes us immune

Open yourself and the rest will follow

Like a shaman finding worth in what's hollow

In each atom there is vast regions of empty space

And amino acids are intrinsically laced

Into a double serpentine that makes your beautiful face

And when unfurled reaches way beyond this place

The length of the DNA contained in a human body reaches
125 billion miles

You can reach Saturn several times

What does that say about each of your smiles?

Lotus Bread

Little peace of Heaven

Right here on Earth

Fermented then leaven

Then she gives birth

Your mind is the Sun

Your body is the Earth

Your spirit is the water washed through the Earth

Until it bursts

Into a photon

Like a lotus with a river to float on

Sunrise on the Frontier

Watching the sunrise on the Mexican border,

a Mexican-American pondering the world order.

Closing off anything is akin to a hoarder,

the natural world has a different order.

The fish and the birds always cross the border.

Tourists try to catch on a camcorder,

but they always fall short of life's disorder.

Her harmony is created by her chaos,

somehow interweaving all of nature's layers.

If you try to build a wall,

the sheer force of nature will make it fall!

Until it finally sinks into the ocean to grow a reef,

according to nature's law.

Extra Ordinary

Your existence is extraordinary

The fact that you are here is absolutely amazing

How many procreations did it take to get you here?

From single cell to your beautiful self

Earth's mountains and valleys

Her rivers and oceans

Formed so exquisitely

That your tribe could live from her breast

And form your own nest

What were the odds that a marble in space would be the perfect
distance from our Father Sun?

And Mother Galaxy

A Milky Way who is so fertile

She gives you the opportunity to look back towards her and
bask in the deep wonder of existence!

Cure your Ignorance

Behind walls we hide

or do we travel wide?

Too much pride when we collide

or do we see beauty in all the Earth provides?

Is your nation the greatest and everywhere else valued less

or is the world great and all the people on Earth blessed?

What's your perspective?

Do you live in a box or are you connected?

Do you feel like your beliefs need to be protected and always
projected,

but when others offer opinions they are unequivocally rejected?

You have a choice to live in a galaxy full of countless stars with

no real borders!

Or live in a tiny box with a limited order.

The choice is yours!

Taken for Granted

Hello world, how are you today?

Still spinning around the deep beautiful blackness of space!

Kaleidoscopic colors splashed around the Earth canvas, as
people on every continent go about their way!

The poles reflecting the Sun's rays as white as snow around a
polar bear's space!

The beautiful brown mud making its way; the deltas are where
the rivers and oceans play!

I can hear the call to prayer in all your sacred space!

I can feel your presence as innocent as children at play!

I can hear you speak a million different ways!

The flora and fauna are illuminating with God's Grace!

It matters not what place, what matters is that the Great Spirit's
Grace inhabits every space!

Imagine if this beauty was lost for all time, what a waste!

Grace will continue to exist even without Earth or humans on this place!

If you appreciate what our host makes, it is time to act with haste!

For the Great Spirit continues creating at an amazing pace!

It is us who have taken for granted this place!

The swells of plastic choking our oceans are a disgrace!

Unmitigated rape of the land happening with no reason except the greedy paper chase!

It's like we are spoiled children who take for granted the parents who create!

What will be our fate?

Everybody Deserves to Be Free

In 1948 there was still state sanctioned hate

Jim Crow was the meat on the plate

White Dudes still had all the power

Black Folk or Native Americans who stepped out of line were
devoured

But not to worry because just over the horizon was flower
power

The 60's ushered in a new hour

Chicanos, Black Folk, Natives, White Folk, Asians and
Women fought to be empowered

Tired of the White Dudes' hegemony, we united and began to
flower

Religion's power took a back seat to a new spiritual age

And every day since we have been fighting for true freedom on
this stage

One where we have the liberty to be who we need to be

Not who the fascists say we should be

Those that try to make this Nation great again with fake liberty

The fight continues against this pedagogy and hegemony, until we are all free!

Regardless of race, color, or creed

Religion or path of spirituality

Gender, belief, or nationality

Everybody deserves to be free!

The Giant No Longer Slumbers

We be the light

In the day and the night

Never succumb to the evil side

Or give in to greed, hatred, or pride

Fascists are defeated with intelligence

Fortitude of peace through God's providence

When bullies use intimidation and violence

We use nonviolent action with internal silence

We stand with Jesus and Buddha

We stand with Rasta and the Lion of Judah

We stand with Mohammed and Krishna

We stand with Galileo and Darwin

We stand with Einstein and Newton

We stand with Lao Tzu, Aristotle, and Socrates

We stand with Plato and Marie Curie

We stand with Tesla and Leonardo Da Vinci

We stand with Suffragettes, Feminists, and Womanists

We stand with Thoreau, Gandhi, Mandela, and Dr. King!

The fascists associate with Nazi ideology

KKK and Neo Confederacy

Anti-science society

Can't you see who painted your hate?

Born with a clean slate then indoctrinated into a state

In which you try to separate

You will not win while we interrelate

We have the power in numbers

The giant no longer slumbers

Multicultural Canvas

In the USA today there is approximately 350 languages being spoken

The voices of immigrants past and present

Our voices are mixed with African rhythm still emanating from Congo Square in New Orleans

From the Navajo mystic chanting right now in New Mexico

From the old English songs still being sung in Appalachia

When that French brother and African brother met along the banks of the mighty Mississippi and had a jam session so epic that jazz and blues would birth a worldwide musical and poetic revolution!

Can you understand my vernacular?

I aim at understanding yours

We are European melodies mixed with the groove of Africa

We are Mozart married to Fela

We are Mexica of Aztlan

Where Nahuatl, Spanish, and English have reached new heights and dimensions

Our love is the sound of:

Irish in New York

Dominicans in Miami

Arabic songs in Michigan

Portuguese in Rhode Island

Nigerians in Houston

Vietnamese on the California Coast

Apache in Arizona

Lakota in Yellowstone

Sharing a Persian meal in your own home while learning a few
Farsi words

It boils down as white and creamy as New England clam
chowder

Or as black and fluid as octopus ink

It is the deep red brown ochre of a Louisiana gumbo

Whether you accept it or not

Y'all Creole

You are the Gardener

Work so your garden can bear fruit

We reap what we sow

To the essence of life we salute

As experience allows us to grow

You are a planted seed

Inside your Mother your heart started to flow

Endowed with your soul's frequency

Your essence continues to glow

Experience transforms the family tree

Evolution is creation in a cycle that is free to learn

Always connected to Siva's creative hands

As well as his capacity to give destruction its turn

Turning life into sands

So that new generations can grow

Never forgetting the sacred DNA code

Your entire history and ancestry ready to upload

Express your genes for your dharma is only your

road

Somehow the Universe coalesced so perfectly

that your beautiful face would show!

Respect the Teacher

All we need is a little respect

Sometimes we only realize in retrospect

Like the soul of Aretha

Singing and dancing with Shakti and Siva

She is our teacher

Taught White Folk and Black Folk to get up off the bleachers

Human beings dancing together and showing respect

Through her music we learned to connect

Even though the mission isn't finished yet

All my bets are on those who don't fret

Those who inherit the Earth,

will be those who learn to show a little respect

Unbounded Education

Flying to the Sun

Playing building blocks with my Son

Youth is learning and having fun

Learning how to think

The only way the ink sinks

Into the mind

Learn to find

As opposed to recite

Figuring out solutions of flight

Thermodynamics is just right for a child's mind

Thinking for themselves instead of following blind

Free your mind

An education you can't bind

Seek and you will find

Get out of the stream of the blind leading the blind

Old Mexico Mestizos

When folks think of Mexico

Usually Aztec and Maya come to mind

But this only scratches the surface of our roots

We can't forget the Toltec, Olmec, Zapotec, Huichol, Raramuri, Chichimeca, Mazatec, Yaqui, Mixtec, Totanac, Tlaxcaltec, Tzeltal, Tzotzil and all those unnamed

In Mexico today there is approximately 350 language dialects being spoken

The intermingling of Indigenous blood with European blood has had centuries to come together

And before their fusion, the Spanish mixed with countless European, African, and Asian blood lines

And now the Mexican-American carries on this ancient tradition of mestizaje!

Mixing in the melting pot, the place where you and I meet

The roots are deep

And the flavor of Mesoamerica is oh so sweet

Old Mother Mexico your history leaves me impressed

Modern Age Latin X

Name Yourself

As I walk through my hometown

My skin reflects the Sun golden brown

Inside my veins a whole history of Aztec and Conquistador

Outside my skin is the present moment's door

Tearing down stereotypes with every step

Tearing down hate with every breath

Sun salutations like the mountain

A spray can is a fountain

Mounting a revolution on the pavement

A canvas for the people to rock the establishment

Hieroglyphs and Petroglyphs

Can you feel the tectonic shift?

Don't let them define you

All together we are one, but there is only one you

Name Yourself

Your spine is like the continental shelf

Knowledge of self defies any category

Paint it with broad brush strokes and tell your story!

Transmutation

Kill the noise

Stand in the storm with poise

Transform negative vibes

Into nutritious meals for the tribe

We thrive when we don't think twice

About lingering with vibes that aren't nice

My soul shield can transmute the vibe's frequency

Makes it into a delicious delicacy

That feeds my soul an energetic meal

How do you think Gandhi did it when the empire thought it
could steal?

Transmute vibes like Mandela in prison

To the snakes we don't listen

We just feed on them

Put your soul shield up and learn to turn coal into a gem

Energy and Spirit

The World is a Classroom

Life is Science and Poetry

We are the Alchemy of this sacred Elixir

Mother Ship

Earth is our spaceship

The Sun dances past her hip

She is a host like no other

Everyone should respect her like their own Mother

Dusk through dawn and into the beyond

She allows us to dream on

Her creatures remind us to awaken

BEFORE ALL IS FORSAKEN

Do not be mistaken

Business does not supersede

Our Mother who seeds

All our endeavors and proceeds

Creative Native

I am a creator

Not just a consumer

I am the narrator

Who can paint you a picture

I am also your listener

To Earth you are a Creative Native

I am interested in how you live

Please give me your art so informative

The uninformed transformed

Education for the soul is born

Art is the storm that transforms

That which needs reform

Breaking norms like Miles Davis's horn

The masters of the past set new standards

Artists are not bystanders to the future we gander

Like Nostradamus and Tecumseh could see

We mix the past, present, and future creatively

Each of us can choose what we want to be

The Age of Mis Information

It used to be hidden

To the masses the truth was forbidden

Esoteric knowledge was hoarded by a few

How the few could create order for the overcrowded pew

Slowly knowledge spread from pharaohs to pharisees

From kings to the aristocracy

Then came power players like the Medici

When the dams were finally breached

The huddled masses could now be reached

Knowledge spread like wildfires

We stormed the Bastille and started to defeat the empires

The people began to be enlightened

Knowledge is the medicine for the frightened

The global market place of ideas is an unlimited field

Look at what a revolution like the printing press can yield

An unlimited field of knowledge revealed

Knowledge travels at the speed of light, but can you handle the load?

Before you upload watch out for the information overload!

Do proper research before you download the show

Every propagandist can now publish without a proper scientific road

Beware of the Age of Mis Information

The Age of Mis Interpretation

The Truth still lies inside an immovable location

Before you make a notation make sure the science had a proper invocation

Most of what you need to know, you all but need to Real Eyes

Decipher fact from fiction and be precise

Knowledge can only be hidden from the uninterested and unenlightened

Those that are easily manipulated and frightened

All one needs is to look back inward

Then carefully proceed onward

Please do not get caught up in the swell of lying idiots

Why would you, when you now have access?

To the masters of their crafts who have gifted us undying classics!

Let your Dogma Go

Does it really matter that I look different than you?

Does it really offend you that I believe different than you?

Superfluous are the mental barriers that separate you and I

If you're bothered by people's choices, then learn to focus only
on your own

Mind your own damn business!

Politic plays tricks to keep the machos whipping out their dicks!

Liberals and Conservatives

Natives and Conquistadors

Gay and Straight

Bloods and Crips

Hippies and Cops

Cops and Robbers

Cowboys and Indians

Israelis and Palestinians

Black and White

Get off your high horse and stop judging

Leave the judging to the Great Spirit

Learn to simply be you!

Live your dharma

Live your own destiny

Do not infringe on other's liberty

It's not that hard to learn to live and let live

However the highest self learns to live in love

Fighting for Freedom

It does not matter your political ideology, it's a bore

Doesn't matter much to me if you voted Bush or Gore

What I am really concerned about is if you believe America
needs to be made great again

When was it great? When genocide of the Native was
happening or when we made slaves of Black Men and Women

When Jim Crow ran the south

Or when Governor Wallace ran his mouth

Or when Bull Connor ran his dogs

Lynching used to be a way of life for these racist hogs

The government flooding inner city neighborhoods with crack

Then locking you up if you are Latino or Black

Don't get me wrong I truly love this Nation

Our Founding Fathers had more than imagination

They put an amazing idea into action

Our Constitution, freedom, and equality became an enzymatic
reaction

In the wake of the American Revolution the French and
Mexicans fought their own revolutions

Still today this original promise of equality for all; is a catalyst
clear across the globe

But it's our present moment we really need to probe

Does the current president remind you more of George
Washington or King George?

Does he carry lofty ideals like Jefferson or resemble a pig at the
trough ready to gorge?

His xenophobia and blatant disrespect to our multicultural
society is leaking into our everyday interactions

Constant distractions while the pigs bleed our environment and
Constitution

Do you believe in this pollution spread about rapists and
thieves?

Make you hate your own brothers all the while the oligarchs
leave only remnants of leaves

We are being deceived by those that divide and conquer

Will you allow this to endure?

Do you side with white power

or a world where the multicultural quilt endures?

My brothers and sisters now is the time, to fight for equality and disavow oligarchy

To find liberty and reinforce democracy

I am willing to forgive

So all our children can live

In a world that Ben Franklin and Dr. King could only dream

Because we are still floating and fighting on freedom's stream

To make sure we never return

to 3/5 of a human being!

Chiefs, Queens, Warriors, and Shamans

Reincarnated in every way

Each generation kills and heals,

but our ancestors never go away.

Ancient smiles on your face

CHIEFS AND QUEENS

WARRIORS AND SHAMANS

You

My loves

Have been all of them

To Forgive is to Love

I love all of you

Each of you

If I have angered you

I beg your pardon

Because love is what I feel now

I hope you feel me

My loves

Life is too beautiful and vast to not spread love

And bask in the love

It emanates from an eternal fountain of energy

Thank you to each of you,

who have ever shown a tender heart.

Shared an empathic hug

or a

tantric kiss!

Thank you for the moments we've danced together

Thank you for the laughter and tears we have shared

Together we have come to the deepest of realizations!

One Love Family

Let's keep rolling

Community keep on growing

I love y'all

Each and all

Even those that disagree

Y'all are rooted with me

In this Great Family Tree

Mama Earth's Dance

Mama Earth in a dance with the Sun and Moon

Our spaceship is radiant from winter all the way past June

Every creature in every corner of this sphere

Shares every move she makes no matter the hemisphere

Step outside and feel her as she invites you in

Secrets so ancient they are about to once again begin

If she doesn't let you in, it's merely your own mental under
your skin

Shit you could easily throw into the recycle bin

Every move she makes creates hurricanes, rifts in valleys, and
the weather you feel now

Pay attention because her poetry is telling you how

Get out that box and learn to caress the princess

You only degrade her, because for you she won't take off her
dress!

Her dress is your shroud

If you really want to hear her

The frequency is clear and loud

Silence

Today in the desert I found life and death

Siva's fist and her breath

Silent for a moment and then I could hear spirits

In full view of the bridge and the force that fills it

Sons and Daughters of Immigrants

I am from El Paso Del Norte.

An old school path on the royal road to Santa Fe.

My ancestors crossed the Rio Bravo many times before the Treaty of Hidalgo.

Harvesting this land even before La Conquista.

Fast forward and my great-grandfather Juan Armendariz immigrated to Texas during the prelude of the Mexican Revolution in 1918.

He gave birth to a son of an immigrant, my great-uncle Albert Armendariz Sr.

In 1954 while serving as president of LULAC he argued at the Supreme Court, Hernandez V. The State of Texas; a landmark case that established Latinos as a distinct class entitled to protection under the 14th amendment.

My great-grandfather Portillo immigrated to El Paso in the 1920's.

He gave birth to Estela Portillo-Trambley, a Chicana poet, playwright, and author.

Her many plays, prose, and poetry depicted the lives and plight of Chicana women in male dominated societies.

The first Chicana author to be placed in the Library of Congress.

My father Lorenzo Mata was born in Juarez, Mexico, and immigrated to El Paso in 1960 at the age of 2.

He has lived his life in the pursuit of spreading education in the borderlands.

He has worked as a teacher, administrator, and professor.

He raised me with this mantra,

"Education is the key, it is the great equalizer in society."

Living proof that the dream is real and the frontera is a frontier!

Go get yourself a proper education, and then see if you can tell me "we don't belong here!"

Sensible Legislation

We need sensible legislation

Like every other developed nation

Our Congress is owned by the NRA

The NRA has roots in those that owned slaves

The Pentagon and Military Industrial Complex

Making too much money to impose mental health checks

We live by the gun

Who cares about your daughter and son?

Perversion of the 2nd amendment

Everyday our CHILDREN'S blood hits the pavement

How many puddles of BLOOD and TEARS

Must we live before we conquer our fears?

Wake up America

Your children are drowning in gun powder

Fully automatic drive thru is getting louder

And it happens everyday

While we say, "it won't happen where my child plays."

Until pop pop pop pop!

Oh shit it's your child who just dropped!

When is it going to stop?

Organize and Vote until not one more innocent is killed by a
cop.

Congress what happened to proper representation?

Get the fuck out the way with your reservations and hesitations!

I thought this was a country of innovation.

Unlock the Mystery

To those that represent hate,

I serve history on your plate.

Only the truth will open your third eye,

I hope this happens before you die.

Do you really want to be on the wrong side of history?

The Great Spirit's creation unlocks all mystery!

With science we evolve and learn,

the secrets of how Allah-God-Mother Goddess turns!

SHE burns like the Sun

and resonates in everyone!

Can you tap into

where every human being comes from?

Earth Drum

Orbiting Solar System

Angels on Earth every one of them!

Mahatma's Footsteps

One love people unite

A war tactic bigger than a fight

Jah children in this war as peacemakers

Even if the other side is filled with violent takers

We can all be together

When we all learn peace is so much better

In flight like a feather

While one is tough as leather

The alchemy is real

Make the choice to heal

Genetics + Education

Our sons and daughters have ancient genetics from the
whole tribe

They will express themselves their whole life

We the tribe get to teach the culture

Live close to nature and choose the pure tincture

Life is ancient and new

I see my son's smile in you

Until the day each of us becomes the stars

Our sons and daughters will travel far

And play the game better than par

Basking in the fact that they are made of ancient stars

Life and Death

We are always on the verge of life and death

Living all the way to our last breath

The limited nature of our time gives it value

As those seconds tick away, you write your story with

everything you do

You bring nothing and you take nothing

As you're leaving, new life is coming

A lifetime that's numbing

Or a lifetime of becoming

Cower in the face of defeat

Or flowering in the face of heat

Everyone you meet and all the vibes you create

Every step you take and every heart you break

Our life's creations ripple through history

Good or bad the future receives this delivery

We are butterflies who flap our wings

And across the Universe we have created hurricane force

winds

Your body turns to dust, the spirit recycles, and your

deeds travel

Every move filled with lust for life's cycles and all the

essences you channel

Transmitting live and direct

Before I die

I want to show you a little love and respect

This life is not perfect

And at the same time has no defects

Enjoy it while it lasts

One thing for sure is that it won't last

And it matters not if you are first or last

One Day We Shall Overcome

I believe we will reach the mountain tops

One day Black Lives will be respected by all cops

Israeli and Palestinian children will play in the streets of
Jerusalem

All this will be hard fought and not in unison

I believe in this vision

The drug wars will recede

And a better future will proceed

The addicts can be cured and no longer need

To be jailed

This war has unequivocally failed

I don't believe we will ever reach utopia, we will always have
problems

But I do believe our present problems, we can solve them

We can awaken and be woke

Only if we move the spoke and provoke

Confront our most pressing demons

Transforming them into beacons

One day Sunni and Shiite will seize to fight

On that day we all will bask in the light

I await the day all the world's women have equal rights

So they can live with dignity as they tuck the children into bed at night

Extreme poverty on every continent can be curtailed

When we realize both socialism and capitalism have failed

Confront the problems that make us grow stale

And find a way out because our coffins don't yet have nails

One day the idea of separate race will disappear

On this day the Human Race will be reborn in the absence of fear

One day Jews, Muslims, and Christians will pray together on the Temple Mount

On this day from our high horse we will dismount

And renounce our massive head count

Imagine the astronomical amount

Of money for war reallocated to solve the problems of the poor!

Open your doors to those that have been ignored

This will usher in a new score and you will be a spore

The long road continues, the least you can do is open your windows

To recognize how the wind blows

Being woke is to understand, "who feels it knows."

Earth Massive

7 billion people

Looking through Plato's peep hole

I implore you to step outside

The light is illuminating the whole tribe

Open the aperture into your third eye

Your experience is the story of life

The human collective is the sum of you and I

Earth Massive

The wounds of history are active

Rumi Says, "The wound is the place where the light enters you."

What are we going to do?

Earth Massive

This moment is active!

Rumi says, "Your heart knows the way, run in that direction."

How Do You?

How do you tend your garden?

Will life grant you pardon

From your transgressions

Karmic lessons

Justice grows in every fruit we harvest

The time, the energy, and the people we invest

We can be stressed and at the same time blessed

I must confess that sometimes this balance is hard on my chest

So I sit back

Take a breath

And in a mantra I express and invest

The sweet milk from Mother Nature's breast

EXPRESSED through the pineal gland

In my head a whole symphony, a whole set from my inner band

Even though I am sitting in traffic

I can see the moment as ecstatic instead of tragic

Her energy is always flowing and never static

Take my next breaths and steps and try to keep my balance

Deep down inside I know the truth is always there, even when I am stuck inside my own palace!

We can always choose to go outside and end our isolation

It's all inside our head

All the while we exist inside an infinite polyrhythmic orchestration!

It's your garden inside a bigger garden that is tended by the greatest gardener

How do you tend your garden?

On the Cusp of Oneness

Love and light

Our sons and daughters shining bright

On Planet Earth's flight

As Luna pulls the tide

Our feet and waves collide

We dance with the sea tonight

Fully merge into one we just might

Fuel Your Inner Fire

What a little imagination can do is remarkable.

We each have an infinite potential within us and when allowed to activate; the possible phenomena are limitless.

Throughout life all people encounter others who cultivate this potential and others who attempt to stifle your inner bloom.

My advice is to surround yourself with those that believe in you.

Folks who want to help cultivate your dreams and goals.

If you must be in the company of those that attempt to diminish or extinguish your highest self, learn to transform their negative vibes into the fuel you need to build your slice of the interconnected pie.

Underground Lattice

After the deluge the mushrooms rise

The ocean falls from the skies

Under the soil the fungi await

Thunderclouds crashing foreshadow their fate

As each drop of the sea moistens the ground

The mushroom can hear as Mother Earth's heart pounds

A symphony so alive and full of heat

Soon the fungi arise to report what is always happening under
our feet

A lattice of fungi connecting the roots of the forest

A network that allows the trees to communicate through the soil
so porous

If you still don't think the Earth is alive

It's time to step outside and receive her vibe

One love and light to the whole Human Tribe

Learn to communicate with Earth, so you understand why we
must keep her alive!

Let It Loose

Do you realize that every sunrise is the prize

The reason to stay alive

All the while in every second the whole world happens

Life is open and adapting

The Earth is a jewel cruising to our Star's gravitational pull

Our Star one of many in a room full

The Milky Way is filled with a plethora of suns, each with
planets of all sizes

Each with their own sunrises

A fertile nest nestled inside a cluster of galaxies

Science is an exploration of all life's possibilities

Our fantasies could prove to be realities

The probabilities in a Universe this vast leave open all
possibilities

Look deep into our Universe and you will count more galaxies
than stars in the Milky Way

Can you fathom the possibility that beyond our Universe there
is a Multi-Verse at play?

We can expand our minds as far as we choose

If you choose to let it loose

Happiness is Born Inside You

Does it really matter if you ride a bike, a bus, or cruise in luxury
wherever you're at?

If you have a 5,000 sq. ft mansion or 500 sq. ft flat?

Or maybe all you have is hard concrete on your back

If you don't have true meaning in your life

Or if you lack love in your life

If you're always searching for this and that

But choose to neglect where real happiness is born at

Happiness isn't born inside things

Happiness is born inside human beings

The relationships and the love we create

It matters not if it's steak or rice and beans on your plate

It's who is sitting next to you sharing that conversation at the end of the day

Maybe you have all the money in the world, but do you have anyone who wants you to play?

Anyone who makes you smile, no matter what they say?

I am not against things, acquire them if you choose

Just don't get so consumed that you lose

The truth in our journey is always free of charge and comes directly from you!

Some people are poor, so absolutely poor that all they have is money!

Picasso lives at Altamira

Altamira Cave in Spain

Where early humans tried to explain

Your home is a blank canvas and a temple

To paint your experience: both spiritual and temporal

Beats pumping from your heart as the endocrine excretes
neurochemicals

On the cusp of flowering like a bud

Paint as ancient as blood

In a human abode

The art flows from the soul's download

"No teacher other than nature," says Rousseau

Budding artists at Chauvet Cave in France 35,000 years ago

In the past leaving tracks as earthy as dirt

As fluid as energy that's never inert

Ochre crayons brilliantly used 70,000 years ago in Mama Africa's Cape

Our Brothers and Sisters transmitting live from their home at Blombos Cave

Art is to flirt with life to birth new bones

To invite life into your homes

Lasting generations like Olmec stones

Wherever we roam we make observations into poems

Like 13,000 years ago, ancient Argentine hands painted

Cueva de las Manos

Art from our bones transforms stones into homes

Like each life is a living poem

Today life gives you paint because 40,000 years ago

Our ancestors laid foundations at Cueva El Castillo

Painting ancient forms like Picasso

Power

The power of your votes

Independence declared with risk to their throats

The king abhorred the idea of the people's rights

So the general and his motley crew started a fight

The red coats are coming tonight

Bombs bursting with light

Light it up and burn it down

Sign me up even if my bones end up in the ground

We won the fight and the right to representation

Representative democracy as a new form of nation

A republic with the people's rights enshrined in the
Constitution

But still only some classes were given the right to vote

Took until 1920 for Women to be let through the rope

Tied ropes denied Black Folk

Until the Voting Rights Act passed in 1965

And still today some find ways to deny

We are still in a fight for every citizen's right

To get to a poll and vote

Now it's division and apathy that is the lynching rope

Get up and vote and engage in the declaration TJ wrote

The road to freedom needs the people to show!

Show we have the power in numbers and it's time for our lack
of representation to go!

Chief Joseph knows!

"The Earth is the Mother of all People, and all People should
have Equal Rights upon it."

The Multitude of Lives

The human body is both perfect and still evolving

Our DNA's ability to weave new cells into organs and the legs
on which we are standing

As we are immersed in our habitat, our system can change the
variables to adapt

Inside we are coded with genetics that are the experiences of
every place we have been at

Single cell organism to your present multitude of cells

Drawing from the water of Earth's wells

Surfing her swells

Walking through her steamy jungles as all life surrounds

Traveling through her deserts in search of an oasis or water
underground

Listen closely as your heart pounds with the flow of your DNA

All life is ever-changing, so our genes have learned to mold clay

Play for a while until we must move and find a new place to stay

I believe that every one of your ancestors exists inside You

They are present in everything we do

Our lives are not solitary or singular, our lives are a multitude!

From the birth of a single cell to every incarnation after

You have been there

The link was not broken it was passed on to the next generation

You are the link, the bridge that connects all

incarnations!

The Yolk of Getting Woke

Stoke the fire to invoke

Provoke

The highest self for the modern age

Filled with the rage of a history locked inside a cage

Educate and turn the page

The printing press set the new stage

Let the knowledge cure the stage fright

Occupy the streets and demand a cure for our plight

The system of injustice is still killing day and night

Let them know we will not stand down till it's made right

Run for office and get out the vote

Vote with your wallet and go for the system's throat

All the people of Earth

Together in the fight for our lives

Black, White, and Brown together is the only way we thrive

Non-violence is the method of this revolution and the reason

we will survive!

Our actions will contrast with those of the beast

The oligarchs will fall when those with the least

Take off the leash and unite in the streets

INHERIT this EARTH through PEACE

We will vote and democratically activate

A new system above the hate

From the ashes the phoenix will rise

The human collective has arrived

Our actions to fix a system that is broke

Is the yoke of birthing a revolution that is woke!

Let's All Bloom Together

In Bloom

A Womb

The Bee Loves the Perfume

As the Dance of Life Resumes

A Catalyst for Your Inner Bloom

Love Will Find A Way

Made in the USA
Lexington, KY
06 December 2018